Unholy Methods

By
Jezebel Crow

Book 1

Don't Call The Cops; it's just Poetry

A note on the text:
This book was typed onto a smart phone tablet, copied and pasted onto social media, then copied onto a word document. I have chosen to publish flawed in text. But the syntax is perfect. I assure you. These poems date from 2013-2015.

Thanks to all of you who made me do this.

Unholy Methods

You were afraid to die alone

So you clung to everyone who

Ever touched you.

Every finger that brushed along your skin,

Every breath pulse that you held someone's eye.

All this human contact

Anonymous or when you came to know

Their name like the thunder of your own blood in your ears.

After a thousand daydreams

After we said goodbye

On that slippery mourning street

In the dirty snow of town,

We parted like shadows in the dawn

We parted like the desolate angels

We were.

I have withdrawn from you a hundred times at least

I know my limits, I know the limits of my love.

Numb and shocked, free and unburdened, drowning all feeling.

Exhilaration and longing,

My unholy methods, and my

Techniques of self love

And loathing.

I've worn my sheets threadbare and torn

Washing you from them.

And then you come back.

I know the porch board's creek

Under your busted boots.

And if you came back now?

Would I slip you beneath my skin,

Once again

Like a desperate needle?

Would I take you into my blood?

You draw the breath from my lips

And do not give it back.

Tonight the coyotes sing the ecstasy of killing,

Beneath bitter winds the trees answer.

The night is edgeless.

Care & Feeding of your Dragon

Foremost,
The dragon must be left alone to roar
Occasionally, yet not extensively.
Do not neglect to polish
Her scales or she will wilt.

It is never easy
For a dragon to let herself
Be stroked by gentle fingers,
Or to even let you approach.
So go slow,
You have no idea what dam
You are about to breach.

Your dragon does not love
You until she shows you the soft
Spaces in her spiky shields.
Consider yourself honored.

Maybe you had no idea
That a dragon could purr, but she will
For you. If you deserve this closeness.

Once she lets you in, please trust her.

 Love is the absence of fear.

Neck of the Woods?
She will show you the rare domain
Of her heart eternal,
Which she carries over
From life to life.
She grows evermore
Strong in its devotion
Through the search for her own
Worthiness to worship. You, lovely.

You will see
Vast expanses of peace, in her hidden lair.

Yet don't forget that your dragon is hot
Her blood is molten copper
And it surges with the moon.
And this Earth

Is the only god she answers to.
This time. Here.

A dragon is a creature of dreams.
If she tells you she dreams
Of you. Know yourself for a companion
In a world more real than this.
Wake her gently.

Take her flying, if she grows grumpy.

Stir her blood to her bones
With your closeness, with your soft words.

And never hesitate to meet her eyes.
Feed her tidbits of authenticity.
She craves radiance
And raw animal protein.

Girdled with Roses

Caught Up In a Moment,

I think of you and my stomach
Drops out.
Kisses make me broody.
The touch of love shocks.
Of all the lost nights
I'm glad I didn't fuck you the first
Time I laid my eyes on the heat
Shimmering off your skin.

Her mouth tasted like a hell lost
To peaches perfectly ripening.
My thighs are gilded,
I'm girdled with roses.
I think of her hands and
The strength of her.

Dawn by dawn
We cast out what is past.
The sea is restless,
I'm breaking like waves
To forget you and dissolve
Like foam into letting you go.
We will all rise again
On the tide.

And so I remind you
I am not straight.

If your car is in a ditch
I'm your servant.
Call me your hero
I'll take it
I cut to the chase.

Launching prayers like lanterns
Sending prayers of gratitude
On the western freshet.
Oh thank you thank you
For rewarding me
For standing upright.

Hoarder of Bottles

In the first liquid of Spring
Sorting the outbuilding lean to
After a tide of snow and dark.
Boxes of bottles blue green bubble glass

Stamped and some even lidded
They were mined
From farm dumps in backfield creeks
Or passed down from moldering
Pantries.

Old green Chianti bottles
With thumb holes for swigging.
Pennies heavily stashed.
Gallon pickle jars
With mead gone to vinegar.
Vintage comfrey salve in bulk.
Squat jars crusted with ancient
Shea butter.
Growlers from scattered breweries.
Purslane tincture from 1996.
Boxes of empty wine bottles
Await the ferment that
Carboys with vapor locks promise.

And here,
An old wooden chest
With hundreds of resin stained
Essential oil bottles
In amber. Close your eyes
And draw the mingled scents in.

Lavender, peppermint, patchouli,

Sage and Cedar.

These liquor bottles
Are being saved to build
Stained glass windows
For a chapel kitchen.
Bombay, Patron,
Frosted vodka fifths.

Outside the trees are bulbed
Permanently with more
Champagne green, cobalt blue.
A stash of purple glass.

A vault of kombucha and
French chèvre culture, kimchi

& sourdough.
Jars of jams and jellies,
Food stacked in Mason mostly
Rice and legumes.
Drawers of tea and herbs.

The weight of accumulation.
Sedentary and still.
Stirring up old story lines.
Drawn in the dust of
Curved glass bottles.
Cleaning with the rain.
That offers itself liquid
Once more.

Breathe For Me

The days grow long,

Dawn comes on,
Still I sleep.
Driving in the soft snow
Singing and crying
Cuz since I first touched you
I've been so sorrowful,
And so blue.Last winter and this,
You're the reason the wind
Is blowing so cold.
Sucked in by the vacuum.
A litany of pain,
Endless letdown.
Not strong enough
To stand my ground
To hold my ultimatum firm.
No effect it's just a bluff
Called. All this circulates like smoke
In these endless hours
Day or night watching
The moon phase past
And it moves so fast
Around a now so slow
I'm a puppet or on auto
Pilot
Awareness surfaces so rare
Piercing the moment,
Stunned by the senses.
A dolphin breathing so brief
Before plunging back
Into the benthos. If I loved you I would
Be fed to think you happy
And warm
No matter touched by another.
If that's what it took,
To make you smile.
I should rejoice
If I loved you
But I don't.

Gravity Points

A woman is born a greedy whole.
She must be taught to crave
Fulfillment in another.

It begins
With your father's denial
Of your beauty
Or his inappropriate attentions.

Glossy magazines dissect
Your self-worth
Or your elder sister's curves
Blossoming ahead of
Your skinny legs
And knobby stick shift
Knees. Undercut
the banks of your riverine beauty.

When your boy friends are
Boy - friends
And you bond over carburetors
And midnight hikes.

Palm flat push on the ratchet
Handle so when the nut busts
Your knuckles don't. Or
Blood through black grease.

You taught me
There's something about the way
Cold beer scratches against
The back of your throat.

You took me to shoot
And to back country meadows
That you must crave
To reach.

You taught me
Love like chainsaw exhaust.
You taught me
That it takes a pig a
Long time to die
Even with a .357 bullet
Just behind its ear.

You were extraordinary in the
Honed edges of your blades.

Handsome butcher. Able mechanic.
Competent carpenter. Farmer of obscene vegetables.

You taught me.

If there was a slacking of time
In the busy-ness of
Self-preservation,
Did I not seek you out?

And didn't you try
To teach me
To be smarter than the cows?
To be complete in my vows?
If I said I'd show,
I'd be there, early.

And all for the love of you.
Sugar king.

And all for the love of you
Vagrant Sailor.
With your charts & maps
All in blue and tan.
Translating to salty buoys.
And anchor chains.
Gravity points.

And all for the love of you,
Slick tanned gazelle.
All for the love
You caught my eye
With your craven beauty.

You who taught me
To pay for my valiant spirit
In blood and bone,
You who made me fight
Just to live alone.

And all for the love of you.
There is nothing you could do,
It's no fault of your own,
Your failure to measure up
To my expectations,
You fell short
Of the price you promised
For one night alone
With me.

A woman is born a needless hole.
Everyone I let close to me,
Tries to fill my vacancy.
Really there is no one for me.
There is no One for me.

Except maybe the rain.
Yeah, I'll take the weather.

Bearing North

I feel you Bearing North,
Pressing down on me.
I feel you pressing
Your presence and bringing the drug
Of your scent back into my breezes.
You know.
It means more to me than it ever did to you.

I was never better and often bitter.
Never better just different.

And I wanted this slick oblivion
I wanted you. Maybe we dissolve
Each other or distill our love down
To syrup sticky sweet.

And all the water boiling to steam,

dripping from galvanized tin.
We strip layers of wool
To feel the rough boards you press me against.

Who are you?
To reach across the silence of my night?
Did my owl allow you
To bridge my oasis?

Wake her gently and devoid
Of pressing thirst.

Of all my lovers.
We never tolerated domesticity
Never the routine boredom
Of maintenance .

I slip you of your fetters.
I break you unfettered.
Both of your wings are strong and feathered.
All knowledge defined.
And everything we knew.

Do you remember
How we sat up around
the solstice fire? We waited
The night unto dawn
Until everyone slipped away leaving us there.
And I shared my blankets with you.

Do you remember
Inviting me home to my house
For coffee and sex and so

You could ask me
Eventually to love you.
With the ferocity of love
You'd not deserve.
Do you remember, lover?

This life is inevitably dawning
Like each night carries on
Into morning. Whether I am sleeping
Or dancing or merely lost.

Give me your eyes.
Give me a dagger I'll sever all ties .
Give me your broken, longing, hungry spirit.

I'll be home. I'm always home.

I'll be the One

I'll be the one
You find sitting in the corner
Where the shadows are as deep
As my eyes.
I'll be the one.

Remember my motion when I move
From your proximity.
Remember your life because
You never needed me.
Oh no.

This girl with shadows for eyes
And I'm doing you no favors
All these lost promises
You belied.
I'll be the one.

You reach for in a half sleep
On a relentless snowy dawn
You refuse to wake up to
So you meld waking dreams with

the heat of your slumber.
I'll be the one.

I'll be the one
When summer never lasts
When all paradise crumbles and fades.
I use my solo hours to stack
Firewood against the relentless winds of winter.

I'll be the one.
You blow home to.
Off the salty, indifferent roads
Of your current journey.
When all hope is exhausted
And you are ready to drop
Your hopes to dreams.

I'll be the one.
To catch you.

Breathe For Me

I woke up this morning

Restless in my bones.

I woke up this morning

Broken & alone.

I'm the one saying,

It's over baby

I can't take anymore of

Your peregrine

Love.

I draw the line

Oh one more time.

I draw the line razor sharp

Fine. I draw

The line in blood

And in tears

I draw the line.

But how would you know?

You thought to cauterize

My wounded heart

To burn the bloody gash

Shut. With the fierce hot

Iron of your touch.

Is it better

A scar ridge risen

And numb?

Better than a weeping love?

I hold steady the

Home stead.

A gift to lower my head

To my work.

And not notice

The world you have fled to.

There is nowhere else.

No land where the rain falls

Gentle and warm.

There is no world

Outside of this storm.

You are nowhere to notice

All these lines I have drawn

Spoking out from my center.

I'm the center of a

Bone yard.

Black holes circle beneath

My ribs.

I tell myself to breathe.

I hear you whispering

Just breathe.

The wind breathes for me.

Lost Cause Angel

I catch myself dwelling

On your broken smile

Lost cause angel

Busted prince of the gutters

Ragged knight.

I catch myself dwelling.

What fallen sky rests upon

Your fragile shoulders?

Who feeds you

And draws you in close?

Smell the smoke of the fire

You sit beside.

It is not sugar maple

Or cedar

Or the birch which I burn.

Lost cause

Ragged angel

Prince in rags

Ghost.

I draw my mind away from you.

I can not dwell.

As I walk the slushy streets

And vague coyote trails

Of my life

As I sit in the same cabin where

I once shared the nights with you.

As I drive these familiar roads

These landscapes embedded with stories.

I hold course.

I maintain the spin

I started well before

I found you

At the midsummer fire.

I layer memory upon memory.

I forswear longing

I forswear dwelling

In all your lies and all your glory

Gabriel I forswear you.

Pierced By Needles

You were a fool to think that you could hold him

Beyond holding him

For the night

For just a moment

And now he's slipped south

And now

you buy your freedom

Breath by breath and night by

Night.

In solitude and in wanting

In company and in in longing

In the spaces pierced by dusty sun beams you dwell.

Though many can find you here

In the vacant spaces you carve out

Between dreams

Between coffee and sleep

You rest your days

Brushing auras with many

Yet untouched in the cusp of longing.

Maybe somehow it's all

Alright. not too many

Moments are pierced by needles.

Only when you need them to be.

As If

Maybe I am

  The kind of girl

Guys get messed up

More by than over.

Why

Would I want

To derail your life

For an hour

Or a year?

After 23 lovers

How could I believe

That you were finally

The one

True

Fated

And destined

Soul mate for me?

As if after all this time

Maybe you could

Make it all alright

With your heart beating

Against my ribs beneath

My breasts pressed

Under your weight.

As if

Maybe your whispers could

Lead me home the long miles

Of gritty road

As if maybe your touch

Could extract the glass

Shards from the matrix

Of my soul

As if you could

Somehow make me whole.

But it all passes

With the spinning of the Earth

As a wheel always finds a center

To revolve upon.

And a new dawn comes

Close upon the heels of the night.

And morning sun casts shadows

As dark as brightness is bright.

So go on your strange journey

And don't let me lure you

Away from your life story.

Every meeting is a parting

Every beating of my

Heart sings.

And solitude is my

Base state

And alone is my

Primary addiction.

And what I need is

To slip into dream

And pass the night

On the waves of my own sea.

So go now

And turn away from me

Winter's Dream

This night

We go beyond

Veils and bridges

That we strike

Like camp.

Bridges don't burn

On these nights.

When the cold

Braces the stars studded

Like tires.

The dirt roads lie

Pristine like ribbons

That might lead us home.

Later when the noise

Subsides

And the fire is

Smoldered to oak coals

Glowing

Like lanterns from afar.

Late in the trough of dreams

Under heavy covers

With a dog

The tin roof muffled

Under snow thick

Accumulating

Flake by flake.

All life is a winter's dream.

Mexico

Woke up with your taste on my tongue.

I was dreaming of Mexico.

In the Winter, any vision

Of the hot sun stops me

Overrides the dream mission.

And I forget.

Everything except the sun's

Sweet caress on my

Dappled skin.

I awoke

And heard your whispers.

In the space between

My neck & shoulder.

Before I opened my eyes.

Urging me on. Breathless.

But the streets are frozen

Today and the trees are bare

Of leaves.

And you are gone.

The Road to Hades

The gates of Hades stand unbarred
To you my Bard. You sang the song of
Salome's 7 Veils. Inanna descended
Arriving as naked as birth.

My love, slow to ignite. Smolders during the night.
Bursts into flame With the breath of your kiss.

My love is a signpost on the road to Hades.
I stumble through the snows of a thousand Winters
To clear my head of the flush of your touch.

I suspend belief, need and interference.
I don't want to mislead another.
Onto the road to Hades. The road to Hades

Pluto take my hand, dark lover.
Lead me to your land across the River Styx.
Wash my mind of trauma. I've been falling into your
Dark mirror.
This is the sweet breath
Of surrender.

All the veils are rendered.
Inanna descended
In pursuit of her lost lover.
I walk this road alone
I wear my skin as my
Only home.

Where are you tonight?
My true soul
With the flaming eyes.
What are your alibis?
I'm coming for you.
I'm tired of waiting.

The Final Tear

I am tearing your dagger
From where it wedged
Against my sternum.
I feel my soul brush against your fangs.

After shock & adjustment
After numb & angry after
Lonely & craving. After
Hope lies breathless.

After disappointment
Calcified my joints and
The fingers of Winter seeped
Into my brittle heart.
After dreaming, after driving,

& cutting & hauling & smashing & knitting skin.

I armoured myself in silver plate studded with amethyst.
Now flashing from a thousand facets. Reflecting
Every assault. Every insult.

I come now to sit alone tonight.
The air still pressing into my lungs.

How to yank these barbs
From my heart?

The skin stretched taut.

A quick tug.

Maybe I Get Choked

Maybe I get choked

Because I have too much to say,

And he wouldn't hear it anyway.

Maybe I'm too much.

Fully present, I warp the space around me

Consciously.

Maybe you wonder

Why I hood my eyes like hawks

And bind them lowered with leather straps?

If I bring them level

With yours I'm threatening

To change your life.

Never for better.

In dreams and without.

Maybe I will hold my business

Up close to my chest

This time.

Assuming me dark from the start,

No one sees my deepest shadows.

This girl sad & sober flashes

No strobe.

When he blocked that light

It was inky beyond.

New Tattoo

The scabs on my heart

Itch tonight

Driving me sleepless

And I want to peel

The wounds open

With my dirty fingernails

Just to sate the itch.

So let the healing begin

They say

Knitting flesh itches

It's to be expected.

What's left to be dwelt upon

When there is no craving

Greater

No book to read

No food to eat

And all my candles

Are burned to stubs.

I lie in the dark

And listen to the dog dream

I try not to feel

Or wonder where he is.

Vampire Butterfly

Under the guise of agape

Lie your lies and apathy.

Butterfly vector

Transmitting infector.

Feeding off of innocent and sweet.

Feeding off of all who you meet.

A predator in an angel's disguise

You rape with your eyes.

You only know how to take

All who love, you eventually forsake.

That you're as shallow as a mirror

It couldn't be any clearer.

Though I said no

You wouldn't let it go.

You said it yourself, you're a cheap whore

Sayeth the Crow, "nevermore."

Blood Honey

You're a wound that keeps

On seeping.

And I try to glue it together

With honey & yarrow

But it gets drenched with blood.

And even though I soak

The sticking bandage

with tepid salt water,

It peels the scab

And bleeds again.

Blood that was recently

Within my heart,

Mixing salty red with

Honey I smear

And dripping down my wrist

Like nothing could ever again be

Sweet & uncorrupted

By the pain of love and bees.

And though scab will give way to scar

And fade

My devotion to you

Goes nowhere.

And the wind rattles the panes

And my solitude

Rattles my pain.

And you're gone gone

Never to return

And lie with me again.

I Never Was a Cutter

I never was a cutter
Until you fucked my soul.
Now I'm soaking dish towels
with the blood of my rage.

And my knives are sharp

You sat there last night
For the last time
Watching me hone my steel
Blade.

Let it out. Let it out.
Release the blood of my heart you infected.

Seven years a soul to cell.
To wash your touch
To fade you to fade

your scars from my skin.

To unfuck my soul.
To stop blaming myself.
To cease craving to cease living.

To shatter and destroy.

Oh you've given me
Nothing but ache.

Nothing but desolation

 To thaw my heart. Just to kill.
Just to kill. Just to never be here.

You never were, you never will.

Taste this love that
You can not have.
Learn to crave my touch.
And I'll give it to another.

You carry the curse of a thousand years.

From these tears I shed.

For this blood I spill.

I will haunt you now.
I will.

Disillusion

My illusion has moved on.

He has taken the artifacts which he entombed here
In this tiny tight coffin
Of a cabin.
With me as a haunt eyed ghost to dwell among.
To pretend he's holding me
When it's just his scent
From where he wiped his dick on the sheets.
To pretend he shelters me
When I'm just a bin
For his dirty socks.

My illusion has abandoned.

Gone are the tawdry trinkets
to dust and snow.
And thawed, the last trace of his breath,

frozen on the glass of the door.

Smashed are the mugs from which we sometimes shared coffee.
On days when he could ever settle and still the fret,

 the restless craving to hunt the empty streets and roads.

 The ceaseless pining for some never present home.

He sat on the black leather couch and chewed his fingernails.
He cut me out of his stories line by line.

You were never mine.

Restless my heart frets
A golden hawk bound
In the cage of my ribs.

Lazy Warriors

"Baby, fuck the world, "
She said, humanity is a lost cause
With all it's complications
And it's derivations.
The work you think you must perform
Daily
 Is eating the biosphere.
And you're doing us all a favor
Sleeping late.

Come sit here beside me
She said
Until you grow restless
And then let's walk the contours
Of forest and field
Until we grow hungry.
 Then let's cook
Food simple and slow.

A fire burns in the hearth
And no duty called
This lifetime
We have no children asking
It's kinder to refrain.
Make your work
 Your self your sitting
Your soul quest
 Work your creation
Quietly within.

Somewhere in the midst of your habits
Your habit your habits
 You inhabit
This sleepy little back woods planet.
Planet planet planet.

Cradled in the womb
Of your habits
You inhabit
This sleepy little back woods
 Planet you inhabit
You inhabit
With your habits
Your habits your habits.
You inhabit.

Breathe in loneliness
Like it's the craving
 In your Lungs for oxygen.

This solitude is your medicine
Take it

I don't care any more
 Our love's a broken door
 And I nail it shut tight
 Trying to figure what is right
 But no matter how many nails I drive
 It always swings open for you wide.

Fake it baby fake it

The boys like me flat on my back pretending I'm still young.
 They like me meek they like the way I take it baby take it.
 I'm untapped potential I'm so strong.
I'll fake it baby fake it
I'll let you pretend I'm spent
 Because I absolutely refuse to depend on you.

Night Watch

When I can't sleep
I don't get up
I lie in bed,
I'm on a night watch
 Instead

Watching the moon
Shift with the slant
 Of it's light

And between
Awake and half trance
I find your ghost
Imprinted on these
 Tousled sheets.
 I have not changed
 Or straightened the tangle
You left.

The wind creaks the trees
As the temperature drops
Again
But where I lay is as warm
As a fever delirium.

On my night watch
Can't escape
Into dreams
 Ragged as my sheets
Heavy as down
Quilts

Reaching for a match
To light a taper
 Is out of the question

Beyond my breath
And the hush of the wind
Lies a deeper quiet
And my ears ring
With thought
Half dreams of touch
And the gaping space
That is tomorrow

After I watch this night
After I watch this night

Slide by like a dark serpent
Etched with moonlight

Curse

What if your curse
Was
 Not knowing if you wanted some one
Until you lay down
In the dark with them?

As in you never knew until
You tested a connection
In comfort and in the silence of night.

Would you ever dare
Invite someone home
 Just to see if
You could love them?
And risk chancing that you could not?
 What would be your excuse?
Would you let them fuck you
Any way? I have.

Would you chance risking
That you would fall
 In love & completely feel
Their touch, only to lose them eventually to tide & time
As you know you are bound.

It's a risky business
And you are doomed to try or sorry you didn't.

Frost Owls

The frost line
Is down 6 feet
Pipes are bursting in the city
Even corpses in their graves
Are bit.

The owls are prowling
Hungry through the gaps
Of the chicken coop.

Last night in the dark hours
Their screams brought me
Up and to the window.
Naked wondering what predator
Was killing.

I fired the .357 out the window
At nothing at all. Shock waves echoing,

I realized
 Everyone must have heard.
 And still the chickens were screaming.

I imagined trekking out to the coop
To wrestle a weasel in my underwear.

But once it's dead, it is food
And why waste a death
And deny what is hungry
It's kill.

So I went back to bed.

Between My Teeth

Loneliness is something
That I hold between my teeth
Like tinfoil
And your proximity
Only makes it worse.

All day today
The north wind pushed
 It's fingers in drafts
 And I burned my weight
In dry oak & maple.

Walking slushy streets
Made my head ache.
I held the windchill
Between my teeth like
Loneliness.
 I was grinding my
 Impulse to touch you down.

Steel and ice.
 Venus brilliant in the western
 Sky
And Mars above,
But only if you knew
To look for him.

Shaken Not Stirred

Return to the scene
 Of a love or a crime

Shaken not Stirred
 You get what you deserve.

Knock me down,
Just don't knock me up.

Thinking we could do better,
We quit each other,
Only to wind up
 Haunting the same bar.

The snow never stops
 as long as Winter lasts.
 Every flake retains it's Self.
 They say each one is unique,
 but who checks?

A Saturday night
Ginger & Rum.
 Who is going to say
How come?

Another night of
 Exile
 Which is doing what I like,
Serving only myself,
No compromise.
Me & I
Til death do us part.

I need a wormhole
 From my cabin to the bar
 So I can fill the wood stove
 So I can not
 Drive the current blizzard
 Drunk.

Run Away Girl

Every black ghost in this town
 Might be you. Walking by
Our lives brushing, eddies in your wake,
 But you won't meet my eyes.

If you never asked anything of me
Then why do I feel so free?

The music is too loud to talk over
I'm more alone than at home
At this evening bar.
I miss you most
When I forget that you were never
Here.

The grind of my life
Is in the simple things
Arriving home to a stone cold
Cabin. Not a coal in the stove.
 And my fantasy
That you'd ever be there
To meet me, the fire glowing.

Maybe twice in eternity
 He met me there.
 And he pined the price away
Fretted the nights away.

I revel in solitude
I light my fire quick and hot.
 Melt goat water on the propane
Unfettered in this world.
 Run away run away girl.

Inside Out

My beauty is crawling with virus.

My body pushing you out in quakes.
I'm alone in a crowd and gregarious in my dreams. I live
Subterranean subcutaneous.

The flower of Venus is defiled with the knowledge of you.
With the blinders down, at last, at long last, all that's left is
Aftershock detox.

My skin is crawling with echoes of your touch,

my ears shout with your ceaseless whispers.
Because you lied, nothing that you ever said holds up to introspection
It's all twisted.

Holding a mirror to my delta, realizing the trauma of skin
Does not cease with your constant dry penetration.

I'm contaminated with a lifetime of your consequences.
Your choices & habits & can't say no,

coupled with your predatory greed
And complete disregard of my health & sanctity will
Be with me every time I'm touched.
Every time I want to.
Every lover who approaches with
Suggestion in his eyes.

I'm the inside out girl.
The don't touch me I doubt
Girl.
Alone in a crowd I'm lost.
My beauty crawls with virus.
And all you say is take more
Lemon balm.

I want to run you down in the street.
To tattoo a warning
Across your forehead.
To save each and every princess.

From the cost of
You.

Love Bitch

I'm made of love
 Bitch
Like I need to beg
For your attention
As if you ever once
Gave more than
You took.

Losing you
Is losing me
Into liberation

Watch me fly
Like an arrow

SubZero Heart

Suddenly I knew
I'd heard all your songs
Too many times.
 I was no longer sad
But liberated
As I split
The cross corner bar
Where you played
That snowy cold
Moon bright night.
After a year and a half
I turned into the wind
Tucked myself close
With once again
Nothing to worry about
But my own little
Universe
No longer forsaken
But liberated.
 No more bow on strings
Emo
The cold numbing my skin
Bone deep
And not sparing my heart.

Toothy Boots

Tonight the roads are
Slick shiny black glare ice.
 So I lace on my toothy boots
And head out drinking porter
To find you
Walking
 And it suits Me
Well

Ducking into the woods
 When cars pass by
 Writing poetry
Beneath the visor of my hat
Dripping rain.
 The rain sheeting down
Illuminated in the headlights
Of the car I'm hiding from.

I walk into my doubts
And embraced by my faith
In you.
 Just at the crest of the view
And beyond the streetlight
I never noticed before,
 At the line of the point
Where I said I'd go no further.
 I see you walking clad in black
And carrying an umbrella.

You came to find me
In my sadness and insanity.
And it is not lost on either
Of us
The irony of my fresh ecstasy,

Stirred by my pulsing blood that I only find
 Here walking in the dark
And the rain on ice
Soaked through my layers
Of wool.
 Laughing smoking drinking
Expounding in the night. I spin on the heel
Of my sharp toothed Boot.

 And we escort Each other home.

Give us

Give us a hundred nights
Or a thousand.
What's a million
To a billion?

Give us these nights

Who trespass
 Against our skin
And sweat
Until clothes
And bedclothes and
Open
And open and
Again upon
Our skin adheres.

Give us
Nights upon nights
Nowhere to shout
Near each other out
We remain a mystery.

Give us one upon another
Each upon each other
In due time my love
In due time.

Altars

The altars which we weave
Together are dark
Knives and hides
Bullets and teeth
Turquoise and quartz
Objects of blood and stone
And stop

Silver encircles bronze
Black tresses and blonde curls.

The altars that we weave
Together consist of dream
Coffee yerba smoke
And blistering cold salt line
 Highway.

Summers we part.

He Got

He got 2 years probation
"For kissing a girl,"
He said.
You said
"To my lover's girlfriend"
And your mother called the cops.

You said
"He's only half a man
 To love you."
And my best friend
Packed her tipi and left
Because I defended
Him.

Rainbow Gatherings
Infidelity & lies.
 I studiously stoke the fire.
 Gather all smashed pottery in buckets.

Cultivate calories.
 Stride out in woods walks.
 Maintain truck, land, finance, homestead.

I can not hope.
To reel me in,
 Or him.
 Or anything wild.

The coyote haunts the edge
Of my nights.

Miles Upstream

Is there something in me that you think you could hold?
Just for tonight,
Do not think me so bold boy
It's not you that I ache for
Not for tonight
My wounds go so much deeper
Back, back to the passage of time
 & beyond.

There are ghosts I have walked away from
Scars I have faded
Bitter moods shrugged off
And you think me still jaded.

Back, back beyond
All the bridges & lights of
This little town, a few
Miles upstream
Maybe there is a quiet place
That you think we could lay
Down together close.

And listen to the rats scratching
The wall boards
 And the snow falling in a hush.
Hush now love.

The stars pierce the cold night sky.
 But nothing matters
Except our shared heat.

The Holding

In the Holding of the year
I walked to the kills.
 The coyote kills
 A spill of blood in the snow.
These deer survived hunting season
Only to succumb to fang.

Every population of survivors
Mutates until the species shifts.
Who among us dares to be famous?
Will we make it,
Will we make it through?
 Dare I say,
Will we survive the rising tide
Of our species?

I've got a story to tell you
If you'd care to listen.

Useless Kiss

And I would tell you
That I love you more than
 Ever
Here at high slack tide,
 A pause before
The waves recede.

I would tell you
I love you more than ever
At the gloaming dusk
Just before the shadows
 Obscure you
 From me for a last time.

I would tell you
That you never know
When a parting will be final
In all of our comings and goings

As if it could change anything
This love we hold so high
And cast so low,
To groveling on bloody knees
Drunk
 To begging for another kiss
Another useless kiss.

I would tell you now
I love you more than ever,
 But love is worthless
You taught me that.

Dead End Lover

I've ridden your rocky waves,
And you have suffered my blows.
Dead end lover.
Love spun of glass.
Everything is transitory.
A second is as deep as a year.
Moon follows moon into yesterday.

We rush about
We keep spinning to remain upright.
Objects at rest fall over
And relationships too,
Collapse inward.
Even the Earth upon which
We rest our foundations
Spins in the void.

Winter Kill

I've been bound now so many times
For love

Bound I am by chains of glass
Looking for something to smash against for freedom
Calculating risk to my wrists
When I shatter
Your spells
This love
This love bleeding
This love bleeding on snow
A wolf's winter kill

A thing bound by chains
Of glass or ice.

Come the New Years
We make the cut.

You've been following him since December

Through the ice
Through the snow
At times you've fallen
Skinning your knees
And bleeding beads of red
Onto crushed boughs
 Of blue spruce
And noble fir.
 Everything scatters
On these primitive roads.
 I keep pursuing night hunts,
Maybe better to stay at home.

Maybe

you will make me bleed
Or you'll call the cops
When I tell you
I cut myself to the bone
And I stand here
Soaking dish towels.
 That's what I say
Before I turn off the phone

But you shouldn't care
Enough to involve the law
If my blood comes from
 The way you fuck my ass
 So hard
Or from this polished silver
Of surgical steel
 I hold in my hand when you defy my love
And leave me here stranded.

Blood is blood
All bleeding is a release

Maybe there is nothing
Between us that could ever be alright
Or maybe we lean on each other more
Than we care to know.

I'm broken you're a twisted soul.

Defying gravity

She'll tell you that she's going to leave this town
  And you will understand.

One night drunk, stunned to epiphany
  You and me
  And all these words echoing from my dreams:

Here I am holding you
Mamma I'm not sure what to do
Here I am holding you
And I'm not sure what
  You want me to do.

This night, the moon set early.
  The bridge is all lit up
And the river rushing
With the late thaw of an early freeze
And no one really knows
Where winter will take us
From here.

The bathroom to the right
Is haunted and you'll never figure
The light.
  We may never know
If its worth even suffering for.

The town is lit with
Blue flashing lights
Tonight
  Be careful driving home.

Hades

We started bringing out the sickness in each other & bailed.

Every vow we spoke was a promise failed.

I held on to you so tight

I cried, wept, & wailed.

You were holding me by the throat over a cliff.

Convincing me brutally of your cold cunning

Your perfect indifference.

I'm exhausted.

Trying to draw a breath not tainted

with your treacherous stink.

Sink now.

You fall.

It's your turn to burn.

Of me you wanted rid.

I abandon you instead.

Oh Texas

I will no longer hold my father against you.
With your 5 acre gas stations and
 A million miles of barbed wire fences.
 And your sweet gentle nights and
Late sunrises.

Please offer me
 More live oak
Datura and
 Nopal

Please offer me
Another night of armadillos
And cheap dressed beer
 That's salt and lime.

Texas grant me another sunny day
I know you've got enough
Even your cloudy mornings scatter
 With the pirated songs of
The Mockingbird
And the heat of the day
Moves off with the breeze
 Scattering with the song of the fiddle and dobro.

Yes Texas, a part of me is yours.
 I surrender to your stars.
 I give it up to your lone star.

Horns

There is too much blood in my veins.
I can feed it to you
Or I can cut myself.
 I just did.
I have learned that it is easy to kill.
Smoother to cut a throat than to saw a board.
 It takes little pressure to press through

flesh with steel honed sharp.
 The mere force of a finger

on the broadside of a blade
Rends flesh & yields blood.

Anyone who has filled their eyes with me runs away.
 The curtains of solitude must remain to obscure me.
 My aloof nature denies pain on my part & yours.
It remains me here bleeding alone this ink,
With no savior on the horizon

and no hope of true lover or friend in this world.

Here I stand naked before you.
It's so easy for me to disrobe.
 All the blessings of this Earth I barely deserve.
 In this life I can barely afford

 to be alone in this madness.
Don't come close out of adoration or pity.

Bad Love Junkie

I'm a bad love junkie & a junkie can't be trusted resist.

Every betrayal sinks you deeper into me
 barbed thorn lover.
You fester in my flesh

and then come back to cut the rest.
 My love for you is heavy clouds

 that block the sun from ripening berries.

I'm left here craving as the days slip by

you deny me your eyes

 you press your skin against another. Lover

Nothing in this world is right since I met you.

I would carve you out like a tumor from my bare heart.

I would not fear the blade if I thought this pain would fade.

You know I can't say no. I can't be trusted to say no.

There is nothing to start with another.

There is no refuge whether or not you choose
To find me here once again in the depths of this night.

Swiftly Deep

I go swiftly deep when you leave me again .

I go catatonic because its always the last

 time you are walking away from me.

I go swiftly deep

 I fall like you asked me to fall

like you pushed me a hundred times.
Pound for pound you've broken me

as much as I've shaken for you.

I go swiftly deep for days and nights

as your touch fades from my nerves

 as your scent from my skin.

I seek remedy for pain in pain.
I cut wood instead of veins.
Instead of ripping my heart

open at your request,

I rip muscles, tendons, joints, and bones.
I chase the wrenching out of my guts

and into my flesh.
When I want to pound my

head against the wall,

I grant myself five pounds

of nails to wail upon.

I'm building a roof to launch myself from.

I'm busting boards to save my knuckles.
I'm building myself a roof to launch myself from.

To fly or fall. To sink or swim.

I go swiftly deep. I go wildly high.

Heart's Warrior

I'm a warrior of the heart
I lay down with you in these tangled sheets sometime between
When you say you've been all the way away from me
And when you swear you will always return to my hearth.

I'm busy not waiting for you in the days between the rain
The rainy days when we have nothing to do
 We do our deep soul work in the hours between sex and dreams

Nothing's lost in the measures of rest

when we find each other again it's always new.

And you always wake with me wondering

what living you're missing while you while away the hours

with your skin on mine.

I'm a warrior for you, brave and willing.

I fight off demons of self doubt to remain open to you.

It's a battle charge waiting here for you.

Refusing to wait for you.

In my fury I see you flinch.

 I see you crumble when you reduce me to tears.

We stay up all night wrestling reasons why we should call it quits.

Call it addiction. Call it fire.

Call it anything but over baby.

Come here.

At Last

1. Our love is a butterfly fresh from its chrysalis that never got to spread its nascent wings. They lie dried & crumpled on its back. Denied flight, a sad maimed thing forced to crawl.

2. I'm building pearls around the grain of pain like the moon builds itself through the sky night by night.

3. When you're here you fret and feel that you are wasting days of your life. And I holler and smash things when you tell me the name of the girl you fucked.

4. After two nights I have to send you away so my other ex lover can come and help me roof. He brings tools and initiative.

5. Later I pace around in emotional agitation. Then I keep working to seek exhaustion to annihilate my questioning why I love you. Why we bother. Why I call you back. Why I hold my heart in reserve for you.

6. I admit I'm an emotional masochist. I choose to love the one who hurts me the most.

7. Your confessions meant nothing to me this time. I already knew. I feel you in my blood.

8. You test the lines I draw. You cross every one.

9. The lines I draw spiral and spoke into a web of tears and denial. In the middle awaits the spider of self doubt. Ready to feast on the maimed, crumpled butterfly of our love. Ready to suck it dry and let the tattered remains fall to dust.

10. The night gathers silent around me at last. At last.

Raw Poem.

I'm caught up in a love that won't let go
A love that hooks and rocks my soul
I'm barren without you
You're the sun on the meadow that waits all winter long

You're when the birds all return
And erupt into song
And who cares if it's cliche,
 You know that I ain't wrong.

So you're gone and I just sit and sigh all night long.
 Or I plot rebellion against my very life
 Without you.

Love is a wound
Love is a conditioned reflex
Love is burning the popcorn
Because I am thinking about the last time we kissed.

I'm here, am I not I still here?
 Facing the dark night alone
I call on the spirit of the wolf
But she shadows me
Back to my den.
If I lie here long enough
Maybe I'll remember who I was
When.

Last the summer light turned to gold
And all the potential of April
Began to snowball
Into autumn.

As day goes down to dusk
So maiden shades to woman.

A thousand times

I thought I heard your footstep on my porch
I sat listening for you.
Though I fought you for it
I gave you your time

This is the last time I saw you:
Walking away away away
Like you were always walking away
In sunshine or in storm
You never could stay, you never were here
You're lost

I can't keep track of your beauty
Anymore. I'll wait a thousand nights

Of this restless craving
Or I'll leave you here at the flea market

Along with the damage you've done.
You could never step in my door again
And we'll still find each other.
We'll fall through the ages
And into each others eyes.

I wanted to die one of those times
When you were inside of me
Completely.
Don't let time take you away from me.
Come straight towards me now.

There's nothing left.

This Fire

I keep finding little fragments of our love & burning them
Like worn socks and packaging.
Out by the fire of many storm's tattered sticks I burn
Your hairbrush and your pocket change

from the last night you spent here.

The last night of June.
I rarely use fire to erase
All traces of a love
Burn bridges burn open rings

As you burned your words right into my soul.

Everyday turns up less evidence.
Even the lighters you left are stolen one by one

In smoke circles &
The flow of people through the porch.

I pitched your motorcycle mirror over the embankment

and now it catches odd slices of the sky
It's not far enough gone from my mind

All those rainy autumn nights

When you rode through sleet

 Just to lay down beside me

Shedding your wet leather at my door.

I broke all of the spells, bullets and green velvet

Crow claws entwined with gold locks

 I broke my word when I said no more.

 I broke "maybe sometimes I'm not sure"

For steely eyed solitude and a low grade ache

That flares during certain songs.

In this fire I burn scraps of your promises

 And memories of your radiant smile.

I burn the avenue through which you won my trust.

I burn your denial. I burn your failing to measure up.

I burn every expectation I will ever place on any man.

I'm a lone planet circling this greedy sun.

I feed it my loneliness and my need for company.

Take this as well hungry fire thief.

My self doubt is enough to sustain

A winter's worth of heat.

 Let the flames engulf the tawdry baubles of desire.

And then I'll feed you this old pair of boots he left here.

All he left behind was an axe.

 I'll use it to bust my freedom

 Into manageable pieces.

Second Hand Fuck

I'm the dark widow
Whom you met at a lonely crossroads
In your life.
I'm a slashed glade
I etched a warning into my skin

Did you miss that somehow, boy?
All wreckage I'm junk yard born

I'm a daughter of the bones alone

I will teach you how to bleed.
My hooks are barbed

And the only exit is through
Once I penetrate you.

Locks

When did I become your girlfriend?
I smashed my fists bloody night after night broke
So many glasses, bottles, and plates in my fury.

Was it the itch
That rubbed off from your skin to mine?
We fucked like it could have no consequence
Rubbing dry sticks together in tinder.

And being shocked at the sparks.
 We fucked tripping & stoned,

Through all seasons as if no one would notice

The way loving you altered the scent of my sweat.

With complete disavowal of each other

Each other every time we parted.

And maybe it was all in your head,

Or maybe it's just in mine.
And why are we still
 Dismantling each other's souls touch by touch?

Breath by breath,
In panted whispers, in sleep, in drunken venting

Or typed word by word when we're craving

Another ending.

How to blow it all up?
To give finality to what never existed?

To untwine spells?

To unbraid our contrasting locks.

Dragon

I spent the entire year of the Dragon
By myself
It's necessary sometimes
That we
Allow ourselves
To come back to our Center.

Now I forge my chains in Silver.
 And I carve red hearts into my skin.

Some nights the Moon fills the frogs.

Descend

And so I let this love take me down completely.
 A lead pipe chained to my ankles, dark water closing over my head.

It takes me down through

Abandoned & ugly.
Trapped, clinging, desperate.
Self destructive, consuming, all or nothing.
I drug myself with food & alcohol.

Fill any desire I crave,

Just to blind myself to the memory of
Your eyes locked on mine.
Last time

You walked away from me into so many winter storms,

that now you are spawning tornadoes and hail.

Lightning flickers and rips my heart.

Winds are pulled in to fill the vacancy left.

 Withinl my shocked sudden valleys.

Sitting on the porch, I look up and the emptiness of the yellow chair

across the table, becomes life's greatest tragedy.

This driveway into this oasis is cut through with dappled sunlight.

I see it catching gold in your hair.

The blood of my heart is full of you.

Each pulse is a reminder of your leaving.

I am raw boned and vulgar.

You dismantle my pride word by word.

 With a surgeon's precision, you cut me out of your life.

I am animal

I am an animal.
Chewing my cud
 In the afternoon sunshine.

Human productivity is a disease,
 This thing you call work
Is killing the planet.

I was the last one
Leftover when
Everyone around me got busy with their lives.

Now
I happen to have a fire
It's burning carbon into the atmosphere.
The smoke is directed toward a goat hide, I tore from a carcass.

Before offering the rest to the coyotes.

All this destruction is distraction.
 What I really want is to sit in the sun & drink beer.
 And the means to do so.

Broken

You tried to hand me my heart back, cupping both hands.

Asking for your skin like a selkie, as if I had hidden it somewhere.

You said you broke the spell that bound my heart to yours.

That all the words you won me with were the babble of a stoned mind.

And still I love you, as I lie here by the light of the two candles we made love by,

and my sheets are still stained by you.

I can't stop knowing that you would be here if you wanted be.

"You're not my dream girl," you said. Your words struck a brand,

white hot iron searing into my soul.

Stumbling outside
I'm your worst mistake, my love falls short.

I'm a tattered ghost girl now kneeling here in grass that has no right to be so beautiful,

I water the meadows with my tears.

Watching you go is all that's left of me.

My once proud spirit has fallen, crushed in the gutter like road kill.

The flies of summer spawn in my wasted flesh.

You were my angel. You lit up my life with your radiance.

I'm a mistake, a dead end, you say. I overpower you,

 but you steal the strength from my bones.

You sever muscle and ligament. You rob my spirit of all meaning.

You had your hands at my throat, cutting off blood & breath,

fucking me hard.

 Why did you release your grip, honey,

why'd you cease your hold?

Change

I'm up in the loft, changing.

Stripped of my dusty traveling clothes and rifling through torn shirts,

Asian silks, daisy dukes, canvas, wool and lace.

The weather is shifting all around me, I must move free,

and shed layers, and add cashmere to denim at the evening of the day.

I'm dressing for you. Though you will not come.
 I'm dressing for you. I'm dressing for the rain, ready to strip for the sun.
 You say I'm an awkward thing, clothed, but quite fine bare.
 I'm dressing for you.

Though your eyes look elsewhere.

Seeking all I will never be, once again or ever.

Gabriel

Your name is a shocking wound.
 Rending my breast heart deep like gauze
Shredded bleeding gasping for life
 As I knew it before
You taught me the love of
Leaving me over & over
Again in whispered promises
Of abandonment & desolation

Your name is a prayer of forsaken vows.
 Your name is my greatest love
Failing to measure up
My greatest offer
Being turned down.

Your name is every flower
 Withering on its vine.
 Burned in my mind.

Clad in leather,
 Improbable in your graces.

Your absence is the night's air with no oxygen left to breathe.

It's every night's mare sweating & festering.

My bones ache for their grave. I'm practicing the depths of my cutting,

 precisely to bleed you out of my blood.

How deep can I gorge myself and still deny suicide?

Gabriel,
 Fire when it's not needed.

 I never knew lonely until I met you

Vanish

I think I saw you this afternoon, downtown.
Sitting on the granite steps of the library.
Dressed in black, hooded.
 I did not let my gaze linger.

I told myself that you were some other tramp,

and busied my vanish.

When it all was new,
 I stood silently behind you at a concert and watched

you wrap your arm around a girl, leaning to hear her words

over the sound of metal music.

Drenched from making love to you in a downpour,
 I stood there convinced that it was not you I was watching,

rather another tall boy with long blonde locks.

Until I saw your feet, barefoot in the mud.

 I stood there, and let every emotion wash over me,

 like an incoming tide around my ankles.
Then I stepped forward and claimed you.

Seasons shift.
 Water freezes and accumulates, then with a day of sun,

a warm wind, and a night of rain, it begins to move.

And the voice of the brook once more fills my lonely night.

Black Bandana Gold Glitter

I see you dressing for a party
 A moody anime pirate,
I tell myself I hate you
 And I do.

I hate you for not being here with me
I hate you for looking long and deep
Into my soul, then turning me down.

For opening me, for conquering me, making me beg,

letting hope barely survive.

I hate you for acting as if I am what you deserve because you failed.

I hate you for The Queen of Swords
And I hate you for The Devil.

I hate that you walked away from me into a dozen blizzards,
after getting up in the morning and leaving wordlessly.

I hate your lamentation and your regrets.
 And your sullen beauty which you taught me to crave.
 I hate your reluctance to be needed, your immaturity.

You let me down again and again.

I hate your motorcycle on my porch and your

 ghost that haunts my cabin, my heart, my dreams.

Every tear I ever cried.
 Every time I ever said please.

She-Wolf

I'm a She-Wolf & I've been your dog.
You kicked me for the last time, Little One.
 I let you close to my blood. I let you into my skin.

Way, way, all the way in.
 Raising my chin, I offered you my jugular.

You threatened to ride me hard.
 Take all I have to offer. I lay it at your feet.

I'm here on my knees, proposing once more.

You treat me worse than a bad luck dog.

I've a glamor of pity.

No one recognizes my power for what it is.
 You think I'm yours to refuse.

I'm sharp as the razor winds, biding my time.

The Moon is in my blood, Little One.
 I am my own shelter.
 I am my own comfort.
 I am blood spilled on snow.
 The frozen season.

Maybe this whole tragic World is a seduction, a painful promise.

It's succulent & deadly, fading always to the edge of your senses.
 The Moon falls dark again.

On the edge of the woods the coyotes howl.
 My urge is to join them.

Oiled Leather & Polished Steel

I've been a misfit for 10,000 years. This is not new.

Somewhere along about your greatest desperation

is where your power finds you. And maybe there is nothing to do,

 but hold it up close to your chest like a lover.

Sometimes there is no cause more worthy than the cause of your own freedom.
 So you walk the margin of things, neither submitting nor speaking out.

Crepuscular creatures creep the line of dawn & dusk.

In the gloaming I sit, drawing my guns and boots around me.

Oiled leather & polished steel.

Life is eternal.

It's always a fading evening

in some dimly lit cabin

on the edge of the forest.
Oh God, won't you please touch me?
Why, God, does it have to be so twisted,

this love we share?
What if I ran into your embrace

like a thousand first kisses?
Maybe I'd not be so mad.
I am spun of the force of creation.

Feel my texture, the warp and weft

of my soul under your fingers
As I rise up to meet you.
I'm a drawn bow,

aimed at the target of your bidding.
How do I feel pinned beneath you?

Succulent and deadly.

Full of the promise of all dark things.
Beware of what magik we invoke

with our friction.

Boar's Heart

Hold my heart like you would hold a boar's heart just after slaughter.
Throbbing and still slick with the juices of life.
This is what you want, isn't it?
You asked for my heart.
You asked me to fall for you and I did.
I fell into a pit of sharpened expectations.
And now you deny me & in my volatility I can scarce blame you.
But understanding does not the bleeding staunch.

Mercury meets Neptune in Pisces

Take one deep breath and plunge down into alcohol & words.

And weird frozen mist blowing the wet roads into obscurity.

You're here, you're there, & back again sitting where you sit, muxing..

The days may be longer, but the nights are so much darker.

I move through the snow. I walk the drifts like wandering the dunes

of the desert beseeching water. Instead I walk dunes of snow calling for hot sands.

I am the ache of love unfulfilled. The season that will not shift.

There is no one to rescue me. I keep my own council.

Cold Turkey

From the outset, I was a drug for you, Sweet Angel. You would ride your motorcycle for an a hour on cold, rainy night, and find me in my candle lit loft.

Shaking the rain off your leather, you would reach out and cup my chin in your hand, lifting my eyes up to yours, "I want to mainline you."
And I would will myself to open to you, soul to soul. It was like falling into myself, and you would catch me. Every time. Sweet Angel, I could feel you wrap your wings around me.

We thought our addiction would be sustainable, mostly because it was mutual. We fed each other ourselves. I neglected my loneliness to be with you. You, being more gregarious than I, neglected everyone else who you loved.

You asked me to fall for you all the way, you pursued my love into all my dark, secret places. You melted my ice palace. You moved into my cabin one motorcycle ride at a time. We perfected the soul fuck. We dissolved boundaries with various keys of medicine that I had saved up over the years. We dwelled in each other's minds and slept forehead to forehead embraced in peace and trust.

When snow began to fall, and the light fell away from the world, I came home to find you huddled in the gloom, and I knew something was wrong. All those loves you let slip away, all those dreams you allowed to die, just to be in my presence, were haunting you. Your motorcycle was on the porch and the roads of your freedom treacherous.

So you walked away and stayed gone. For months I tried to make it better. I offered you patience, sympathy, rage, and tears. Now I have nothing left to give you but silence. I've let hope die. I sleep once more in the arms of loneliness.

Love Junkie

What's it take to come off this junk that is your love-fix:
 A dozen daffodils and a banjo.
 Memories of old loves from last millennium.
 A six pack of bitter IPA.
 Internet porn.
 Takeout sushi.
 Sentimental music from a woman with gravel in her voice and an acoustic guitar.
 Compulsive spending (albums, dresses, stockings, ancient astrology texts).
 Refusals,
 Refusing all company except your absence.
 Occasional trembling when I get too high.
 Finish carpentry.
 A project car.

Sunshine on my skin promising frog song.

Book Two: Latter Day Poems

Triple Crown

In the soft sweet hours of yesterday
I made love to my Angel so familiar
So unwilling to be held
For long. Then
I dropped him off
Downtown as I always will.
I Threw in a load
Of laundry, grabbed
Second coffee and watched
The springing streets.
Full of the promise
Of mud.
The farm boy tracked me
100 miles north and found me
Where I sat.
So we drank beer while
My clothes were drying.
Then he followed me the rest
Of the way
Up to my cabin.
And gently mauled me
With his love.
After he left.
After not speaking too
Many words.
And after walking the dog
And feeding the goats
And changing my clothes.
I drove back downtown.
And met an old friend at
The bar. By happenstance.
And the music was loud.
To spare him an hour
Drive over the gap.
I let him crash at my place.
And we cuddled without admitting
It all night long.
I'm a Triple Crown
Lover.
Come & go.
As you wish.

Vault

This time
I want to hold my cards
Close to my chest
But I fret.
You've been loosening the bonds
But it's me who slipped away.
Sometimes unbound is unbinding
And the pages scatter
In the wind.
Why apologize for beauty?
I won't ask you anymore.
Even if forever alone
I choose another.
I will sit this darkness
One more night
Knowing I must dig a grave
Come morning.
You never have given me a
Moment's respite from your longing
Heart so I release.
Not angry yet passionate
I bleed change.
In the vault of my refuge
I pace the night. I pace my breath.
I pace the fires and their coals.
In the vault of my heart
Even echoes are muffled.
A friend is a shoulder
To lean on. Maybe your bare
Shoulder is the first
Place they touch.
Using your tattoos as a gateway.
They enter your skin
And then your history.

Thaw

Your kisses left my lips
Swollen and the Earth throbbed
To life. Open wide
we slept with the window
to the rush of the brook
And breezes temperate.
All day long I lay stunned
Under the caress of the sun
I lay resonating with harmonies
Of your touch. Suspended in dreams
Wondering what creeks
This gushing spring would feed
Into rush.
As the snow melts to slush
As Winter's brittle fingers
At last released their grasp
On the earth
On my hearth
On my heart.

If I Were Locked

If I were serving
Solitary and had not a pen
I'd write poems
In my head & hold them
To mind.
I know.
I have spent many a Winter
Alone.

Climbing a mountain
I sing the phrases
As they arrive
And repeat to imprint.
Building word upon word
I speak them to the wind scoured granite
They tangle like lichen
In the alpine scrub.
I fling my sentences
On to the thermals
And watch them rise like ravens.
Swooping deep into the valleys
Of my life,
So that when I am lost
In the decadent forest,
The echoes will ring me home.

When you are inside me
I press my lips
Where your neck meets
Your shoulder
And bite back the words
Which spring from the deep.
I hold them
I hold them behind my
Eye lids.
I let them sink in.

Obsess

I tell my self
Repeat do not dwell
On nights past
Even if he
Untwined your
Mind
When he slipped your
New silk down.

Let him go
When he goes
Say not a word
He'll be back
You know.

If you think
To reach out
If you crave his skin
And search
The pillow he slept upon
For traces of
The scent of his hair.
Do not tell him this.

Draw your shadows
Like a night shawl
Draping your angular shoulders.
Let them brush against
Your skin.

If you hold your self
Like you hold your breath
And wait
For the moon to phase to new.
He will come
Breezing back to you.

I tell myself
Keep many irons
Glowing orange hot
In the heat of your own fire.
Lick the flames
If you are lonely.
You never taught him

To find his way
Without following.
So do not listen
For him.

Strange Fever

The moment I let go
I was no longer dragged *
So high I was cast
Against the velvet banner
Of the night.
The city became a switchboard
Spread out below.
My senses heightened felt
Your whereabouts but my proximity
Was overwhelmed with beauty
And music and seductive things to drink.
And I opened wide.

In the midst of the glow
I sought a dark corner to sit
And think and to watch
The people move. To try to breathe
To write these words
And not lose track of the jeweled
Prism of mind in moment
Consciousness
Bending time.
I pressed a moonstone ring
Into his palm.
The sky was every color at sundown,
The pavement radiant with the heat of the day.
Because the seasons will always move,
 there is no point in holding on.
To what is lust. Love. Projection. Sustaining. Damage.

His departure opened a vacuum
Here in my heart and so much love
Rushed in. Still I sit and pen these words.
And so if you sing
I will be still.

The door I am closing
Is heavy and dark
The hinges are rusted and
Protesting.

Can I tell you
That your touch stunned me?
It did.
I was shook for days
Shook down to my roots
And I stood for it.
I will let one night altar my life
If that's what you offer baby.
But not before I ask for another.
I have a strange fever now.

Spring Storm

I drove across the night
East until the pink sun rise
Promising myself your caress
As if I held the title.

There are words for your words,
For your begging off.
I call it simply, "the conversation."
I have heard it so often
It's almost a joke.
If a joke could invoke
Lifetimes of misplaced sorrow
And desolate tears.

I don't know love
But obsession
A fever from friction
Fire from contact
Skin against skin.

I soaked your touch
Into my bones.
For a breath
And then I left you
Alone.

As if the belief in new love
Could break the winter
There was sun
And heat in my life
For as long as I believed
In you.

I drove across the mountains
Dodging falling branches
Ripped from the maples by the wind
Skidding on the ice
That glazed my heart.

The Meaning of Lapis

He said
You look like
You've been in the mud.
I agreed.
It's been rain upon
This earth
Newly thawed
And so raw.

It's not your fault
It was brief
We went in fast forward
Played it out abruptly
You shocked me
Into alignment
And it was me
Driving away from you.

Did you hear the words I spoke?
Will you remember my touch
And how good I smelled
Close up and unbound?

As self preservation
I thought I'd try
Not fucking anyone
Who I hadn't known for at least a year.
I've known you for
Four.
I must trust.

There are so many people
And so much love
In this world.
Why return to stand
In a grave?

Too much for anyone
Is the onslaught of my fierce gentleness.
The diamond of my consciousness focuses
The laser of my attention. So I hold
No blame for vacancy.
On your part.

The wind of the storm
We conjured spilled
Maple blossoms red as blood
Across the cold asphalt
Of my morning road.

Fall Line

Craving your company.
Left alone I resort to dreams.
An avalanche of inspired ideas
Journeys and grounding closeness.

What's left after the avalanche?
Silence muffled and echoes that the landscape absorbs.
And eventually the sun
Melts a trickle from its shine.
And portulaca blooms improbably
From the fissured rocks.

Here, beneath my soles
I trace a path which leads
Me back beyond back
To you.
My feet know the groove
Worn into the Earth.
No light is necessary,
But the crescent Moon helps.

What were you thinking
When you came here to me?
So open and pure.
Resolve. Dissolve. Break
Apart & Wait. Wait. Debate.

Fall back as you will
Upon the line.
Upon the fall line.
Devine.

Bolt

Spike spike, double spike
Blow away on the wind
Begin
Begin to live again.
The Earth comes alive
With the first breath of thunder.
Lightning feeds her Nitrogen
Because he loves her.
The World is spun of longing.
Appetite moves all life,
Call it addiction if you must.
Gravity is desire circling in orbit.
You admitted that no one ever
taught you
How to breathe.
Love is born of the storm
And it never dies.
So the creeks swell and rush
With new rain and old snow.

Excuses

Excuses
I'll be your love bank baby
You can call on me
When all your accounts are
Overdrawn.
I want to know that the King Stag still favors me.
I am a warrior of the heart.
And I will walk until god
Speaks to me.
On a day that nothing is moving
Except the water
I'll send you pictures of waterfalls
In lieu of love notes.
Or if you don't deserve
My love I'll crawl until breaking
Until the skin of my knees
Is busted from the gravel
Of groveling.
This is my benediction
This is my grace
I'll let you go back
To standing in your grave
I'll be here leaning into darkness
Alone the whole night long.
I find peace
About a mile downstream
Where the trout pool among
The roots of the banks.
The voice of the brook
Babbles love songs to me,
Love songs ceaseless.
Who among you could love me
With such abandon?
You are always putting your flesh first.
Your greedy needs pushing
Into the sanctity of my love.
And I'll love you
For all I'm worth.
Who can take me as I am?
So scrappy and vulnerable.
I'm a broken hero.
I can feed you
And I will kill in your name.
And I'm also busted
And exhausted. Do you understand

I have no one to fall

Back upon?

All this night it's me sitting here.

Alone by the soft golden flicker

Of 3 candles.

Oh it is so beautiful baby.

So beautiful and tragic and solitary.

And it breaks

Like the waves in my dreams.

Cured

Don't let me convince you
I won't hurt you I will.
The first night you tell me
That I smell good
The second night you touch me
After the third you don't return.
Oh lover of leaving
Oh lover of another
Broken & bright
With eyes like pools,
Why follow me home?
A night as clear as crystal
After the candle light.
Maybe you are devine
You bore into mine.
I'm not looking
I'm not looking
I won't watch you
I won't care where you are
I won't hear you confess
Your attachments or
Your struggles
Obsessions it's not me
You follow.
It's not me you're up against.
I'm not the one you long for.
You do not belong.
The blues catch me broadside.
I breathe though. I breathe.
I say I'm not jealous. I'm not jealous
I'm cured. Cured like leather
Broken like a hide.
I'm going to hide.
Slip off outside
Trace the road back
To the silence of the forest,
Pull my cabin around me tight.
Call it a night.
Don't let me convince you
That I won't hurt you
I've got a nasty bite.

Crush

I crush like a fever.

You won't wake up the same.

The sheets are coiled & damp

Your hair knotted

Maybe for a heartbeat

You can't remember

The night before.

Don't worry boy

This happens every time.

Souls entwine when barriers drop.

We were up all night

Whispering & giggling

By candle light.

This happens precious time

I find one worth bringing

To my bed.

You're special indeed one in a million,

But this happens every time.

If I let you touch me once

It's ongoing in my mind.

This happens every time.

Don't worry pretty boy

Every time.

I won't tell you

That you've worn a channel

In my mind.

I won't tell you my dreams.

It happens like this

I don't bide my time

I jump right in.

All the way is all the way.

I won't hold back.

Every time.

I'm all in. Every time.

Feral Love

In a tree
On the edge of the meadow
The kestrels are mating
They are not quiet
About it.
Did you expect me to court you
Feigning indifference?
It's doubtful, might as well
Tell the roses to tone it down.
Hush your beauty, cease
Wailing love songs, wolves in the night.
This heart is dauntless
Like a ripe plum,
It is meant to burst open
And drip nectar.
Plumb these depths baby.
Draw the wild air from my lungs
When you put your lips to mine.
Taste my boundless affection.
A folly to try and bind
The dance of two souls
With words or vows.
A flowing river festers behind
Locks.
Everything wild paces a cage.

Made in the USA
Middletown, DE
04 July 2023

34520000R00064